Perrie

Jesy

Jade

Leigh-Anne

WE LOVE LITTLE MIX

By Sarah Palmer

Published 2012.

Pedigree Books Limited, Beech Hill House,
Walnut Gardens, Exeter, Devon EX4 4DH

www.pedigreebooks.com | books@pedigreegroup.co.uk

ISBN 9781907602795

£7.99

Contents

8 Fact files

14 Why we love Little Mix

18 Rise to fame

24 Going live

26 I like LM because

30 Fascinating facts

34 Girl talk

40 Make-up masterclass

42 Famous fans

46 Favourite things

54 Super style

60 The Little Mix quiz

62 Papped!

66 Horoscopes

70 The girls on each other

75 Spot the difference

77 Quiz answers

Perrie

Perrie

Full name Perrie Edwards

DOB 10/07/1992

Nickname Boho Mix/Bam Bam Pezza

From South Shields

Favourite song Call Me Maybe by Carly Rae Jepsen

Dislikes When you're trying to fall asleep and someone switches the light on

Before Little Mix Perrie was a student and a waitress

Dream job before Little Mix Vet

Pets Four Huskies, two cats, two gerbils, a snake, a hamster, a pony and a one-legged budgie

Fave food Chinese and Nandos

First album she bought S Club 7

First celeb crush Aaron from S Club Juniors

Most annoying habit according to her She shakes her legs a lot when she's sitting down

Random! Perrie does a really good impression of a goat

FACT FILE

Jesy

Full name Jesy Nelson

DOB 30/09/1991

Nickname Swagger Mix/Wilma

From Romford, Essex

Favourite song Bust Your Windows by Jazmine Sullivan

Dislikes Burping

Before Little Mix Jesy was a barmaid

Dream job before Little Mix Beat boxing/singing/dancing

Pets None – she doesn't like animals

Fave food Nandos

First album she bought Spice Girls

First celeb crush Bradley from S Club 7

Most annoying habit according to her She takes the longest to get ready

Random! She's a big fan of TV presenter Jeremy Kyle

Jade

Full name Jade Thirlwall

DOB: 26/12/1992

Nickname Cutie Mix/Edna

From South Shields

Favourite song I Want To Hold Your Hand by The Beatles

Before Little Mix Student/entering singing contests

Dislikes People eating with their mouths open

Dream job before little mix Singing

Pets Her mum never let her have any pets so she had a beetle called Berry

Fave food Lasagna, biscuits, chocolate

First album she bought Spice Girls

First celeb crush Nick Carter from the Backstreet Boys

Most annoying habit according to her She's a total perfectionist when it comes to the girls' harmonies

Random! In school she had rubbers thrown at her in lessons until she stood up and sang

FACT FILE

Leigh-Anne

Leigh-Anne

Full name Leigh-Anne Pinnock

DOB 04/10/1992

Nickname Fiery Mix/Betsy

From: High Wycombe

Favourite song Only Girl in the World by Rihanna

Before Little Mix Student/waitress in Pizza Hut

Dislikes When people leave bags sitting on tables

Dream Job before Little Mix A singer

Pets A pug called Harvey

Fave food A bit of everything

First album she bought Busted

First celeb crush Aaron Carter

Most annoying habit according to her She makes a weird noise when she itches her throat and the other girls hate it!

Random! Leigh-Anne would love to go shopping in Harrods to buy some clothes for her dog Harvey

WHY WE LOVE LITTLE MIX

There are a million reasons to love the Mixers, and here are some of the best ones!

They still get star struck!

The girls still get excited when they meet celebs, and Perrie said of Simon Cowell, "Meeting Simon was like waiting outside the principal's office. We felt like naughty schoolgirls and were all so scared that we could hardly breathe."

They've got amazing taste

The foursome are seriously stylish and instead of just copying trends, they wear what they love and what suits them. "We wear what we're comfortable in," says Leigh-Anne.

They love their fans

The girls adore their fans and appreciate all of the support they give them. "We get nice books that people make, full of pictures. Lots of lovely letters – it's really nice," says Jesy.

They're genuinely best friends

The girls say that although they bicker every now and again, they never have proper arguments and any disagreements are forgotten in a flash. They reckon they couldn't live without each other now!

They've stayed friends with their old X Factor crew

They may be No.1 pop stars these days, but the girls have still stayed in touch with their fellow X Factor contestants. They all hung out together on the X Factor tour and are still pals. "We still speak to Marcus, The Risk and Craig – all of them really," explains Jesy.

They speak their minds

The ladies aren't scared to say what they like when it comes to, well, just about anything. Take Jade for example! "What I don't like in a boy... is a monobrow. Why is it there? Please, if you've got a monobrow, get rid of it. It's not attractive."

They still can't believe they won The X Factor

Even now, Perrie and co are in shock about their win. "I don't know if it will ever sink in. We prepared ourselves to go every week and we were prepared to come second," says Jesy.

They're amazing role models

"It's sad when you see celebrities getting drunk and ending up in rehab. We're not like that and won't ever be," says Leigh-Anne.

They're individuals

The girls are determined to stay true to themselves and be happy with who they are. "If everyone looked the same it'd just be boring," says Jesy. They've also got different tastes in music, but have the same ideas when it comes to their sound.

They want girls to be happy with who they are

"I think it's good to look curvy, whatever size you are it's good. Girls come in all shapes and sizes," says Perrie.

They're kind

The first thing they did when they won The X Factor is buy their family some lovely presents for Christmas. Bless! Let's hope we all get one this year, eh?

They weren't the cool girls at school

"I was always the one at school nobody fancied and I've only ever had one proper relationship," Perrie has admitted.

The girls are so close they even wear the same boots!

LITTLE MIX'S RISE TO FAME

They were the first girl band ever to win The X Factor, and they've got a massive future ahead of them. Here's how Little Mix rose to the top!

In 2011 four girls entered The X Factor as solo artists, hoping to achieve their dreams of becoming professional singers. Perrie Edwards, Leigh-Anne Pinnock, Jade Thirwall and Jesy Nelson popped along to various auditions around the country, and were left heartbroken when they were turned away as solo artists during bootcamp.

However, the judges had bigger plans for them and the girls found themselves being put into girl groups and being given a second chance. But it was only after another rethink by the judges that the four ladies ended up performing together as a four-piece.

They won a place in the Judges' Houses round, and spent the following weeks rehearsing together constantly in a bid to get themselves ready. They bonded as friends, worked on their harmonies and picked the perfect songs to show off their voices. Then all they could do was cross their fingers and hope that they could do well enough to make it to the live shows and be in with a chance of winning.

The foursome jetted off to Greece to perform for the groups' mentor Tulisa and her helper Jessie J, and were over the moon when they were picked as one of Tulisa's final four after singing Big Girls Don't Cry and Cry Me A River.

Audiences loved the girls from week one when their performance of Super Bass blew the competition away.

The girls got better and better as the weeks went on, and while their fellow bands The Risk, Nu Vibe and 2 Shoes sadly got eliminated, Little Mix continued to shine. It soon became clear that they were in with a good chance of scooping the incredible £1million record deal.

The ladies scored their first No.1 in November 2011 when they performed on The X Factor charity single, Wishing on a Star, and landed their first Little Mix No.1 thanks to their winner's song, a cover of Damian Rice's hit song Cannonball.

In early 2012 the girls joined the massive X Factor tour and started work on their debut album. They've got huge plans for the future, and we don't doubt they'll be around for a very long time!

The band are still close to their mentor Tulisa

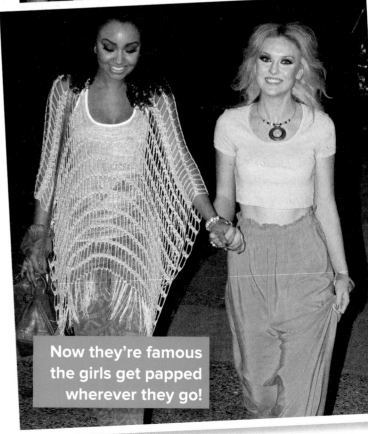

Now they're famous the girls get papped wherever they go!

Little Mix are in huge demand for TV and radio shows

LIVE!

1

2

3

1 The girls' career is literally flying

2 A passing bee has caught Jesy's eye

3 Jade's robot stand-in fitted in very well

4 The superglue on the hand trick gets them every time

5 Jade flies the flag for Britain on, er, her braces

I Love Little Mix Because...

Write down your fave facts
and fun stuff to keep forever!

I love Little Mix because *They are cool!*

I first started liking them when they *sang.*

My favourite member of Little Mix is *Perrie*

I think *Perrie* is the best singer

If I could hang out with Little Mix I would *go to the pub.*

If I could give the girls any present, it would be *Nedass*

If I got to have a movie night with any of the LM ladies we
would watch *Little mix!*

If I saw the girls in the street I would Say come to tea.

The Little Mixer who is most like me is Perrie!

The funniest fact I know about the LM is

I couldn't believe it when I found out that Little Mix sang.

The Mixer with the best style is Perrie.

I love Perrie make-up the most because Love you

I would make a great pop star because I am a so cool.

I really hope that in the future Little Mix is stl alave

DID YOU KNOW?

Facts about the girls you didn't even know you needed to know!

1 Perrie has a scar on her stomach from an operation she had when she was young. As a result she doesn't like showing off her tummy.

2 Jade thinks her figure is boyish so she doesn't like showing it off on the beach in a bikini. We think she's gorgeous!

3 The Wanted are big fans of the foursome and think they're hot, hot, hot.

4 Jesy is a huge fan of vintage shopping and loves finding something new and exciting that's actually old and exciting!

5 Perrie would love to work with Steve Perry from Journey, who she was named after, but she doesn't think it's going to happen. Boo!

6 Leigh-Anne loves any top that has Rihanna on it, and has built up an amazing collection of Rihanna-printed togs!

7 The girls are desperate to collaborate with their X Factor mentor Tulisa on a track. How amazing would that be?

8 The girls deleted their personal Twitter accounts because they thought it would be easier to

6

keep fans up to date from a joint account

9 Jade would love to work with Professor Green in the future.

10 A fan once took a piece of Perrie hair. Goodness knows what they were planning to do with it!

11 Jessie J's a fan and says, "I'd love to write for them as they're great girls and have brilliant voices."

12 Jade and Jesy got bullied at school. Jade says, "The people who are like that are people who see you doing well and they don't like it. It's the same as Jesy now, they're seeing her doing well and they think 'how can I put her down?'"

13 Perrie eats Polos when she meets celebs so that her breath is sweet when she talks to them!

14 Mel C reckons the girls are amazing and says, "Little Mix could be even bigger than The Spice Girls. Plus, they've got an added bonus in that all four of them have equally amazing vocals. With The Spice Girls, vocals weren't our strong point."

15 John from Jedward has got a big crush on Leigh-Anne!

16 Perrie got so star struck when she met Matt Cardle she ran away from him! "When he was on the show, I used to rewind him and listen and rewind him..." she admitted.

17 Perrie hasn't got any sense of smell, and hasn't had any since she was born. We wonder if the other girls help her to pick out nice perfumes to wear?

GIRL TALK

The Mixers have said lots of crazy/funny/sweet things. Here are some of our favourite quotes!

Perrie

"Some guy had a tattoo on the back of his hand. It was a really cute love heart with a 'P' in the middle. Another fan made an album with all the songs we'd performed in order. It was sick!"

"I have to do my own shopping without my mum helping me. My shopping bag is full of chocolate cake."

"I've never eaten a goat before. Does a goat just taste like lamb?"

"My mam would give us a slap if she saw me in my bra in a magazine."

"I like biker boots too... I just need a motorbike now!"

"What's the difference between a washing machine and a tumble dryer?"

"Don't worry, be hippy."

"For some reason when I fancy someone I try and be all girly. Even though I'm totally not."

"We just can't be sexy!'

"I'm not going on a diet, I'm not trying to lose weight, because your insecurities are what make you different and if everyone looked the same, it'd be boring."

"We can't be doing with any of this diet rubbish, so we're just going to stuff our faces."

"He (Gary Barlow) absolutely hated me. I remember wanting the ground to swallow me up!'

"For every bad comment, there are 100 nice ones."

"If someone I like walks past I turn into a shrinking violet. I act like I don't care."

"When I was younger I got bullied about the way I looked and I thought once I was older it would stop. I hated going to school, but didn't know who to talk to about it."

"I think the thing with us as well, is we're all different shapes and sizes and I think that's why a lot of girls can relate to us."

Jesy

Jade

"If the four of us all lived together the place would be a total pigsty."

"The good thing about getting called the Little Muffins – you get a lot of free muffins."

"When I fancy someone I get really loud. Like I start shouting 'YOU ALRIGHT?'"

"We're living out of a suitcase. We each have ten suitcases that follow us around, which is just the worst thing — all I want to do is hang up my clothes."

"My security people are always checking up on us to make sure we're eating healthy, so when they're watching I eat bananas, satsumas and vegetables. But when they're not looking, I eat chocolate. And biscuits!"

"I like boys' stuff so I love Labrinth's style and Bruno Mars' with the bow ties and braces."

"I like One Direction because they're really pretty and stuff. But I like a MAN."

"I've been singing since I was nine. It all kicked off in primary school when I did, 'Ooh stick you, your mama too, and your daddy.'"

"The first thing I do when I fancy someone is blush."

"I never thought I'd have a pair of trainers with my own name on them."

"The best part about working in Pizza Hut? Free pizza."

"I fancy JB out of JLS."

"Style icon? Rihanna. I love the bright colours and her whole old-school vibe."

"The thing about us is that we said in the beginning, we're always going to stay who we are . We're not going to change. We've all kept our own styles as you can see. We're all individual in our styles."

"Because we wear such thick make-up on stage, when we sweat under the lights it makes our skin really bad. You have to try to eat healthily and get enough sleep, otherwise it can get out of control."

Leigh-Anne

BIG BEAUTIES

The girls always look gorgeous and glam, and here's how you can too!

Eye eye

The general rule with make-up is to have either a bold lip or a bold eye – both can equal overkill! If you're going to go for smoky eyes, keep the lips nude and simple with a pretty gloss. Jade uses Sleek and Barry M eyeshadows.

Get lippy

Likewise, if you want to paint your lips in a bright shade, stick to just mascara and a bit of eyeliner on your peepers. Jesy favours Bobbi Brown and MAC lip colours.

Lash out

The secret to the 60s wide-eyed look? It's all about fake lashes. There are some amazing ones on the high street you can use again and again.

Crazy hair

All the girls have dyed their hair wild tones at times, and you can copy their looks by using some fab spray in hair colours that wash out easily.

Don't be afraid to go *au naturel*

Some sound advice from Jade… "Every day we get photographed without make-up, but we are normal girls. We are going to have ugly days but we scrub up well on stage but we also want to be normal and natural."

Let your true beauty shine through

As Leigh-Anne says, "The way I see it is if you don't like me without make up then you don't like me. This is who I am." And look how good she looks!

FAMOUS FANS

Celebs love Little Mix and didn't seem to be able to stop tweeting about them after they won!

GERI HALLIWELL

"Good luck and remember 'Girl Power.'" Geri also sent them flowers!

NIALL FROM ONE DIRECTION

"Yes yes yes yes! Yeeeeaaaahhhhhh buddddiiiie! Congrats little mix, doin it for the groups, love them, Jade's a little cutie."

DIANA VICKERS
"Wooo littlemix! You can tell Tulisa has worked her tush off for them. Congrats!"

TULISA
"what do ya do after ur act wins the xfactor?...go 2 ur local kebab shop of course, wooooiiiiii....LOVE U LITTLEMIX keep it real."

KELLY ROWLAND
"@littlemixoffic!! I know you guys have an amazing future ahead of you... Well done, ladies, and great job @officialtulisa!"

GARY BARLOW
"This is just the start. big congrats to @officialtulisa @LittleMixOffic."

These Are A Few Of Their
Favourite Things!

Waffles, trainers and Will Smith are just a selection of Little Mix's favourite things...

Perrie

Talking in an Australian accent She likes to keep the other girls amused with her Aussie twang.

Johnny Depp He's her dream man.

American waffles She adores the sweet snack.

Nicole Sherzinger She reckons the singer is stunning.

Tulisa's cooking! The ladies loved being invited round to their mentor's house for dinner during X Factor.

Burping She burps pretty much anytime, anywhere!

Sleeping She admits to being the laziest Mixer.

BRAVEHEART

J-LO

WAFFLES

Jennifer Lopez's bum She says she'd swap it for hers any day.

Rock'n'roll She loves a bit of soft rock and was a big fan of rock week on The X Factor.

Braveheart She loves films and calls herself a movie dork. Braveheart is one of her absolute faves.

CAMDEN MARKET

LORRAINE KELLY

Jesy

Trainers Jesy owns 68 pairs!

Nandos She's a big chicken fan.

Bagels She loves toasting them for a quick snack.

Lorraine Kelly The TV presenter reminds Jesy of her mum.

Cher Lloyd She was super-supportive when Jesy was being bullied online.

School Of Rock She adores the film and its star, Jack Black.

CHICKEN

Woolly hats She even wears them when it's warm!

Impressions She's always trying to mimic Jade and Perrie's accents.

Camden Market She loves picking up quirky vintage clothes.

Holly Willoughby The TV presenter's supported the girls since the beginning.

Being tidy According to the other girls she's the one who keeps things organised!

JOE MCELDERRY

BEYONCÉ

Jade

Labrinth She's got a bit of a crush on the Let The Sun Shine singer.

Blue Doritos She likes pouring them into a bowl and munching them.

Dancing She used to teach dance classes before she was on The X Factor.

Being well behaved She was Head Girl at her school!

Joe McElderry He's one of her closest friends.

Disney films She can spend hours watching them over and over again.

Lasagne It's one of her favourite dishes. She also likes sweets!

Cliff Richard Jade admits the old crooner is her guilty pleasure.

Napoleon Dynamite The mad movie makes her laugh 'til she cries.

Beyoncé The big-haired diva is her ultimate idol!

DORITOS

Leigh-Anne

Justin Bieber She dreams about going on a date with the Baby star.

Trainers She especially likes ones with her name on!

Jim Carey The rubber-faced comic is her favourite actor.

Her Pug Harvey She even posts pics of her cute pooch on Twitter.

Making tea She likes to play mum by making tea and cleaning for the other girls.

Pizza She loved eating free ones when she worked in Pizza Hut!

Being an auntie She's got a sweet little nephew called Kailum.

Crazy hairstyles Who can forget the time she shaved off half her hair on The X Factor?

Titanic She still cries every time she watches the classic film.

Nice eyes She says every boy she's dated has had pretty peepers.

Writing music She used to write her own songs and sing them on karaoke when she was young.

JIM CAREY

PIZZA

TITANIC

STEAL LITTLE

They may be called Little Mix, but the girls are BIG on style

ADD ACCESSORIES
All the girls make sure their outfits look individual by adding funky, fun accessories. Jade reckons, "I just think sometimes, that the littlest items make an outfit."

GO CASUAL
During the day you'll usually find the girls chilling in sweats, denim and lycra. Leigh-Anne says, "It's not really a case of impressing anyone, I just feel good about myself and really cool in them."

MIX'S STYLE

GO INTO COMBAT
When asked what item she can't live without Jesy said: "Mine's a pair of army combat trousers – three-quarter length ones."

DITCH THE HEALS FOR HIGH TOPS
Jesy is rarely seen without her cool high-top trainers, and the other ladies also embrace the comfort!

STEAL LITTLE MIX'S STYLE

BE A PRINT-CESS
Jesy is the queen of the bold prints. She's not afraid to express her personality through her togs.

EXPERIMENT
As Perrie says, "If someone walks down the street with a different style, you automatically look at them and think 'wow', they have got guts to wear that."

PUT THE BOOT IN
Don't be afraid of masculine boots like Dr Marten's as you can make them look fabulous and feminine by mixing them with more girlie clothes, just like the ladies do.

BOW DOWN TO BOW TIES
Jade is a huge fan of braces and and has worn them since her X Factor days. She says: "I like my braces, and my bow ties, and a bow in my hair." Perrie also loves topping off her outfits with bows.

BE INDIVIDUAL
Wear what makes you happy. "If you have got your own individual style then go for it and don't let anyone tell you it's wrong. Embrace it," says Leigh-Anne.

The big Little Mix quiz

Think you know everything there is to know about the girls? Test your knowledge here.

4 Who is the oldest member of Little Mix?

5 Which rock star is Perrie named after?

6 Which member of the band had auditioned for the show prior to 2011?

7 What was the band called before they changed their name?

1 Which well-known restaurant did Leigh-Anne used to work in?

2 Who did LM beat to take the X Factor crown?

3 Which TV host is Jesy's guilty pleasure?

8 What did Tulisa cook the girls when they visited her during The X Factor?

9 Which of the girls owns a one-legged budgie?!

10 Who once had rubbers thrown at them in school?

11 Which Mixer used to be in a dance troupe?

12 Who used to have a pet beetle called Berry?

13 What was Perrie's dream job before joining Little Mix?

14 What was the name of LM's first single as a band?

15 Which girl's nickname is Betsy?

16 What did Jesy sing at her first audition?

17 Whose nickname is Edna?

18 Who has a strange habit of shaking their legs when they sit down?

19 Who hails from High Wycombe?

20 Which Mixer is a talented beat-boxer?

ANSWERS
ON PAGE 77

PAPPED!

Everywhere Little Mix go, photographers follow!

Even at a fancy do, Little Mix are always on camera alert

The girls could pose like pros right from day one

Jade perfects her wistful camera look!

Jesy avoids gazing at the paps' flashbulbs

IT'S WRITTEN IN THE STARS

What does your fave Mixers star sign say about them? Guess what? We're telling you!

Perrie Cancer

Element Water **Ruling planet** Moon **Stone** Moonstone

Those born under the Cancer star sign can be rather confusing because they like to change their mind a lot! They're great fun to be around because they love to laugh, but if they want their own space, everyone needs to stay away! Just like a crab they can seem tough on the outside, but inside they're sensitive and kind and can be easily hurt.

When it comes to career, they love to live life to the full and once they set their mind on what they want to do, they don't give up until they achieve their dreams.

However, work aside the thing that matters most to Cancers is love, and they're never happier than when they're in a relationship. They have loads of charm so people are drawn to them and they meet the right person, magic happens!

Jesy Libra
Element Air **Ruling planet** Venus **Stone** Opal

Librans are known for trying their best to stay happy and positive, even when things around them are proving tough. They have an amazing ability to pick themselves up and carry on when things are difficult, like Jesy.

Their downfall is that they're not very good at saying no to people even when they want to, so they can find themselves in frustrating situations when it comes to work. That also makes them a great friend because they will do anything for anyone – but they expect the same in return!

Love-wise, they can be hard to work out as they come across as elusive, but they secretly dream of meeting their perfect partner and riding off into the sunset. When they do, they'll stay with that person forever and are 100% loyal.

Jade and Leigh-Anne Capricorn
Element Earth **Ruling planet** Saturn **Stone** Garnet

Like Jade and Leigh-Anne, Capricorns are very ambitious. They want to climb to the top of the career ladder and make an impact. They sometimes work way too hard and need to make sure they have the right balance in their lives, which means going out and having fun with friends whenever they can.

They love to laugh and are sometimes seen as eccentric because of the unusual way they view the world. They often see things around them other people don't notice!

They're not the types to have casual relationships and they think long and hard before making a commitment to anyone. But when they do find the right person, they are solid and reliable and will do anything to make their other half happy.

Little Mix on Little Mix

They're best mates, so who better to talk about each other than, er, each other?

Jesy On Jade and Perrie
"Jade is the little cute one, Perry is always the last one to get out of bed."

Jade on the ladies
"We're always like a unit. Especially when it came to song choices and stuff."

Jesy on the band
"We're so close, we're like a family."

Leigh-Anne on the other girls
"The thing is, we were lucky to have each other. Because if we didn't have each other, we'd have all crumbled."

The girls on each other
Jesy "If I had to sacrifice anything it would have to be Perry."
Perry "I'd sacrifice Jade."
Jade "I'd probably sacrifice Leigh-Anne."
Leigh-Anne "Jesy."

Perrie on Jesy
"Jesy in the group is the one who will well up. She gets a bit emotional in the group sometimes."

Jesy on Perrie
"She eats, like, the world and never puts on a bit of weight. I have to sniff a bit of chocolate cake and I put on a stone."

Leigh-Anne on all of the girls
"I feel like I'm the mum. I do the washing, I cook…"

Jade on the others
"If the four of us all lived together the place would be a total pigsty."

Perrie on Jade
"Someone grabbed Jade's arm at our concert the other night and shouted, 'I want you!' She just kind of screamed and ran on to the stage. We all burst out laughing."

Jade on the band's image
"I like the idea that mums are watching us and thinking we're good role models."

Jesy on her bandmates
"The best thing about my life now is being with these three girls. Literally, I couldn't live without them."

Jade on the ladies
"I know we are not perfect yet. We don't wanna be perfect since then there would be nothing to learn."

Jesy on the band's cool attitude
"We're very focused, so I don't think arguing would have come into it. We always knew what we wanted."

Perrie on the ladies – and men!
"The strangest thing recently is having guys at concerts who are interested in us. At the beginning it had been all girl fans, so we're not very good with that kind of attention yet."

Spot the difference

We've made five subtle changes to the two pics below. Can you work out what they are?

**ANSWERS ON
THE NEXT PAGE!**

Quiz Answers

Are you a Little Mix superfan or a superflop?
Find out how well you did in our LM quiz!

The super-sized Mix quiz

1 Pizza Hut

2 Marcus Collins

3 Jeremy Kyle

4 Jesy

5 Steve Perry from Journey

6 Jade

7 Rhythmix

8 Goat curry

9 Perrie

10 Jade

11 Jesy

12 Jade

13 To be a vet

14 Canonball

15 Leigh-Anne

16 Bust Your Windows by Jasmine Sullivan

17 Jade

18 Perrie

19 Leigh-Anne

20 Jesy

Spot the difference

1 Perrie's hat is missing a face!

2 Jesy's sock stripe has changed colour

3 Jesy's rings have disappeared

3 Jade's wispy curls are missing

5 Leigh-Anne's buttons have nipped off